This 'n That

some tips, some insights, some computer skills for us older folks

Volume 1

*A small collection of blog posts and mini-tutorials on
Windows Live Photo Gallery, Windows Live Spaces, and Windows 7*

Ludwig Keck

This 'n That

some tips, some insights, some computer skills for us older folks
Volume 1
A small collection of blog posts and mini-tutorials on
Windows Live Photo Gallery, Windows Live Spaces, and Windows 7
Ludwig Keck

Illustrations:
Cover Photo: Justin Keck
Post on page 33: NASA photo S125-E-006596 (12 May 2009)
All other photos and screen shots by the author

V1002

ISBN: 9-781-450-58320-6.

Website: ludwigjkeck.spaces.live.com

Introduction

Dear reader,

Thank you for picking up my little book. For some time I have regularly found myself answering questions with "I wrote a blog on that" or reaching over to bring up a post. So finally, I decided to print out a collection to keep close by for reference. This modest volume is the result. I hope it is as useful and helpful to you as it has been to many friends, students, and readers of *This'n That*.

The posts are reproduced largely the way they appear on the Internet. The blog layout had to be re-adapted for the printed page. Of course, I had to replace all links with addresses that are more detailed. Some of the illustrations do not work as well in black and white. One in particular was the illustration for Windows Live Photo Gallery black and white effects. For that, I reprocessed the picture as the main cover illustration. There were a number of typos that I corrected; I hope I have not introduced others in their place.

The book is organized by subjects rather than date of posting. The first section contains articles about Windows Live Photo Gallery, posts on Windows Live Spaces and related online services follow. Take a look at the contents pages for the complete listings. If you have a question about a specific subject, please use the index.

The *This 'n That* blog site is at **ludwigjkeck.spaces.live.com**, my site illustrating online albums is at **ludwigkeck.spaces.live.com**. Note the single letter difference. Some other sites are cited in the book. Several of those are part of the demonstration sites of Senior Academy textbooks (see **senioracademy.org**).

To get in touch with me, please use the "Send a private message" command on my Profile page at either Spaces site. Your comments and questions are most welcome.

Ludwig Keck

Contents

Windows Live Photo Gallery

Moving photos from camera to computer

6/30/2009

When importing pictures from your camera you have many useful options with **Windows Live Photo Gallery**. After plugging in your camera to a USB port and turning it on, you get the AutoPlay dialog, one of the options is:

Using this option makes your picture management really easy. The next dialog looks something like this:

Do accept the default option to review and organize your pictures, just click **Next**.

Now comes the nice part, the next window looks a bit like shown here.

There may be several groups listed. They are grouped by the time the pictures were taken. You might have pictures taken at different occasions and there may be some time elapsed between these occasions. The import program looks for major gaps between picture groups. Note in the illustration here the photos are grouped by the three different days on which they were taken.

You have control over the grouping. Note the "**Adjust groups:**" control at the lower right. This allows you to adjust the time interval between groups from a half hour to just one group.

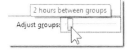

The settings can be made in half hour intervals from 0.5 to 6 hours, then in 1 hour increments up to 24 hours, next in day increments to 30 days, with the final setting being "**All items in one group**". So you can set it to group the pictures in the most appropriate way.

For this illustration I have set 2 hours between groups and that

resulted in four groups.

Now when you click on "**Enter a name**" a text entry box allows you to enter a folder name for that group of photos.

There are many other options.

Note the the check boxes in front of the groups. If you un-check one, that group will not be imported. Also note the "**View all ... items**". It shows how many photos there are in that group. Click on that command and you will see thumbnails of all the pictures in that group. Each one has a checked box and you can un-check any photo that you don't wish to import.

You can assign tags to the groups and define "More options" – but let's leave those for another blog.

Click Import and the folders will be created and the photos copied from your camera into those folders. During this operation you will see a dialog similar to this:

The "**Erase after importing**" box is not checked by default. If you want to clear the photos from your camera, check this box. Here I checked it. Then after the

photos are copied the erase operation will be performed:

After the import chore is completed Windows Live Photo Gallery opens.

More on moving photos from camera to computer

7/6/2009

Has this ever happened to you?

You find that different photos have the same name. This can happen whenever your camera starts over with its numbering scheme. Some cameras do that automatically when you install a new memory card or even after you have moved and erased the pictures. You can set your camera to keep using the next sequential number, but even that will eventually come to a "roll-over" after it reaches 9999 or whatever the camera's maximum number is.

How to get unique file numbers

To make you file names and your folder names unique, make the date part of the name! This will also help sort the files and folders by date – they way most of us think of our pictures.

Windows Live Photo Gallery provides a number of options for managing folder and file numbers.

Click **File**, then on the drop-down menu click **Options**. In the Options dialog window click the **Import** tab. Now it will look like shown here. These are the default settings.

Click on the button next to **Folder name:** and select **Date Taken + Name** – of course, you might want one of the other options.

Similarly, make the selection for **File name:**

These settings will "stick", you will not need to do this each time. With these settings your photos will be named like as shown in the next illustrations.

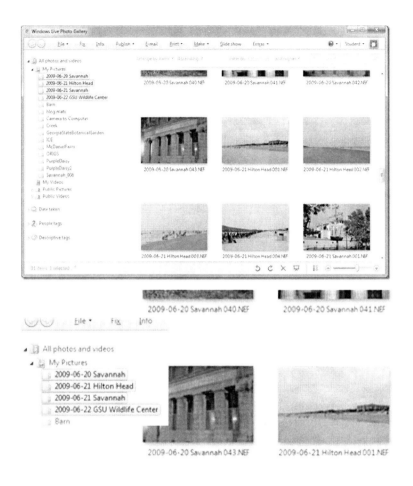

Note that both the folder names and the file names for the pictures will start with the date year-month-day. The name of each photo starts with the folder name and is followed by the exposure number assigned by the camera. I like mine that way. I move a lot of my pictures around, and this way I will still instantly know is "source". Choose the method that suits you best.

By the way, if you have already opened the import dialog you can still get to these options. In the lower left of the windows click on

More options

and the same option dialog opens.

Organizing pictures with Windows Live Photo Gallery

4/22/2009

Windows Live Photo Gallery is a great tool for editing, enhancing, organizing and sharing pictures. Most of the time the program does just what I want without selecting any options. So much so that I don't even think about other settings. Maybe that is how it is with you. Here are a couple of ways to make organizing pictures a little easier.

After I have imported pictures from my camera I like to go through them, deleting the bad ones, and converting the ones I wish to share into JPG format. Oh, you are new at this? OK, a quick refresher:

Plug in the camera, AutoPlay comes up, select **Import pictures and videos using Windows Live Photo Gallery.**

There will be a number of options – a new folder is created and the pictures are transferred to that folder. WLPG opens and you are ready to go. I like to double-click on the first one so it is displayed big. If I don't want to keep it there is the ✕ in the bottom toolbar to delete the picture. If I like the picture I make a copy in JPG format. That is **File – Make a copy… –** set **Save as type:** to JPG and give the picture a new name, although I usually accept the default.

Then I make a new folder for the originals. I drag the originals to the new folder. This is where the default settings don't work out so

well. By default, WLPG shows the pictures in the selected folder as well as the sub-folders. So the picture does not leave the main viewing pane. Besides, the thumbnail pictures do not show the file name, so it is hard to select the ones I want. Here is what it looks like:

So, here is what to do:

Right-click on the folder name (not the sub-folder). The menu offers some options, the last one is **Select without subfolders**. Click that.

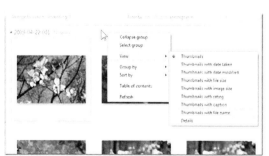

Next, right-click in the main pane top area. Then select **Thumbnails with file name**.

Now you may want to reduce the size of the thumbnails so you can see more of the pictures. You can use the slider control in the lower right.

Now you can identify the pictures easily. Select one, or more, of the ones you want to move and just drag them to the sub-folder name.

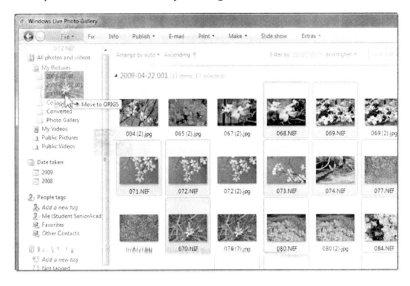

I then edit the remaining pictures. That may include cropping, adjusting exposure and color, straightening the picture. Whatever I think it takes to make them into masterpieces.

Of course, I want to share them, so I select **Publish – Online album...** Then the folder they should go into. And off they go.

Rescuing bad pictures – using the histogram

4/30/2009

Modern digital cameras are amazingly smart. Yet at times you get a picture that misses the mark. Here is an example of a photo that is underexposed – it looks dark and muddy.

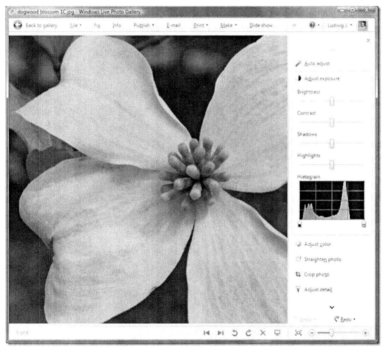

When you click on **Fix** and then **Adjust Exposure** you see the various controls and a histogram. The histogram is that little graph. It shows the distribution of the pixels from the full black one on the left end to the full white ones on the right end. The more pixels of a particular brightness the higher the graph at that point. For this picture you see two peaks in the histogram. The lower peak on the left, dark, end is from the darker background behind the blossom. The high peak is produced by the white flower petals. Except here they are not white but rather gray. Note that there are no pixels shown for a little stretch on the black – left end, and none for a rather longer interval on the white, right, end. The picture contains no real black or very dark areas and no full white pixels. That is why the picture is rather dull looking.

Now there are a number of ways to make this into a better photo. **Auto adjust** almost always does a fine job. With this picture it would improve it greatly. You can also use the controls for **Brightness, Contrast, Shadows, Highlights** and others. Here I want to tell you about the controls right below the histogram display. See the two slider controls, one at the left bottom corner and the other at the right bottom corner of the histogram. Note the left slider has a black square in it and the right one a white square. With the white point control you can set the full white point to any point along the graph. Same with the black point control.

Since the picture has no really white pixels, we can slide the white point slider to the left to just where there are pixels. These will become full white. If you move the slider farther to the left all the pixels to the right of it will become full white. Not normally a good idea. As you move the sliders you can see the changes right there in the picture.

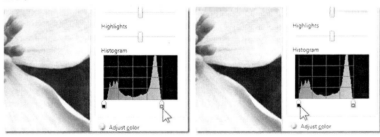

As an exercise for this blog, I have also moved the black point slider up to the first dark pixels. This sets the darkest part of the background to full black. As always, they important thing is to experiment. The best result is the one that makes you happy.

When you are satisfied that the picture looks good to you, just go back to the thumbnails to see if there are others to improve. **Windows Live Photo Gallery** will save your settings so when you look at it the next time the picture histogram will be stretched out fully like here.

To fully appreciate these controls you need to experiment with them. Enjoy!

Artificial wide-angle photos –ICE

5/26/2009

There are times when you find yourself in front of a awesome, overwhelming scene that you just have to share with family and friends. Occasionally the view is just too big, too wide, or too tall to be all taken in with your camera. It might be a palace in Vienna or a mountain valley in the Rockies and you just want it all. Your friends with their fish-eye lenses (and the eighty-five-pound camera bag) just smirk and capture the shot.

So can you!

How? Same way you eat a sandwich, one bite at a time – but I am getting ahead of the story. There is a marvelous "extra" for

Windows Live Photo Gallery called Microsoft Composite Editor. Let me demonstrate. My expense allowance for this blog wasn't quite enough to take me to the Alps or London so I settled for my county park. Here is the problem: This old barn won't all fit in one picture. It cannot all be captured in one shot. ***However, it can be done with many of them!***

So shoot overlapping pictures, right and left and up and down. I got carried away a bit and took twenty shots, but that's ok. Better to have more than you need.

So next to **Windows Live Photo Gallery** and in **Extras** to the neat and marvelous **Image Composite Editor** . Don't have it?

Click on **Download more photo tools** and work your way to Microsoft Image Composite Editor. Download it and let it install. Restart Photo Gallery.

Now in Photo Gallery select the pictures you wish to combine into your wide-angle picture. This time in **Extras** you now have **Create Image Composite**. Click the option and the editor opens in a new window and processes the selected pictures.

Now the fun begins. When the Image Composite Editor has processed the selected images it presents the result.

ICE offers a great deal of control over your composite. Note in the screen captures here how you can "shape" the picture. I won't go

 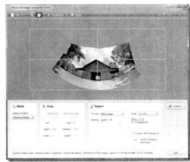

into details here, it is just too much fun to do yourself! When you have the picture the way you like it, you can crop it or let the editor do an auto-crop. Then "export" the picture. Here too you have a range of options over size and quality. In not much more time than it took to read this blog you have your wide-angle shot. And you have more control over it than your friends with the fish-eye lenses.

Just for fun here is another example to show that you can even do it with pictures taken looking down: First the normal shot and then the final wide-angle composite.

Find your photos 1 – By folder or date

8/31/2009

Once upon a time – actually not so long ago, but before digital pictures – when I wanted to find a photo I went to the closet where I kept my **Pictures** and started to go through boxes, albums, **folders**, and envelopes. Some of these I had marked, some still had the labels from the photo shop showing the date they were processed. It was a chore. Now, with digital pictures and **Windows Live Photo Gallery**, finding a specific picture is much easier. On the computer there is a "closet" called "Pictures" with "boxes" called "folders" where most of my pictures are kept. Photo Gallery locates all these pictures all by itself.

Before going into the details of locating a specific picture, you may wish to make sure that all of your photos are included in Photo Gallery.

I have some other places on other drives that Photo Gallery does not locate automatically, some of these are external drives. You may have some of these other places too. It is easy to tell Photo Gallery to find those pictures also. Here is how:

Click **File** and on the drop-down menu click **Include a folder in the gallery...**

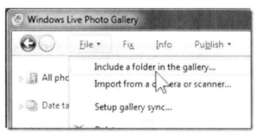

A new dialog allows you to access anything on your computer. Click **Computer** to see all your drives. On my machine I have a drive called "Home". There are a lot of pictures there. To include a whole drive – not really a good idea – just click on the drive name and then on **OK**.

You get an option to change your mind. Click **Add** if you really want to do it. Photo Gallery searches the location for pictures and they are displayed.

Click **OK** to close the dialog that tells you of the deed.

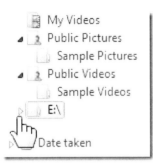 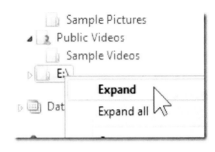

The folder, or drive, will now show in the navigation bar on the left side of the Photo Gallery window.

You can click the little arrowhead in front of it to expand it. If you have trouble moving the pointer to that little arrowhead, just double-click on the folder name or right-click on the name and click on **Expand**. Now you can see all the folders or subfolder. There may be some that you really don't want to include in Photo Gallery. So quickly, how do you remove a folder from

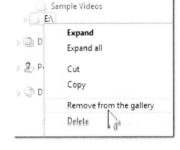

the gallery? Easy. Just right-click on the folder in the navigation bar.

A warning: You can't remove a subfolder of a folder that you have added to the gallery. So be sure to individually add the folders you want. You can remove any folder that you have added this way, but not a folder inside such a folder. Similarly you cannot remove the folders in you **Pictures** library or the **My Pictures** folder.

Now that you have maybe hundreds of pictures in your gallery how do you find any one?

Well, your pictures are organized pretty much the way that hall closet was. In the navigation bar there is **All photos and videos.** When you expand this listing you see all the folders and subfolders (not all folders will be expanded). In my gallery it looks like the illustration here. Pretty much as gruesome as opening the door to that hall closet!

But everything is all there. The main display in the gallery starts with the first photo. The folders are shown in the navigation bar. If you imported your photos and took advantage of labeling and dating the folders, the organization will be neat. I am not that organized myself. Still all the folders are there and organized within each folder alphabetically by name.

To see the photos from any particular folder just click on the folder name. If you have subfolders, you can expand the folder listing and click on a subfolder. If you know your organization, you can find most any picture. Well, my memory isn't all that good, I don't recall what I labeled a folder. As you can see, some folder names just don't make any sense at all. "New80410" what brilliant idiot came up with that? Ops, sorry, that was me.

Now sometimes you might recall about when you took a picture. Oh, that was on our vacation last November. Photo Gallery can find your photos by the date they were taken. Most digital cameras record the date and make that information part of the data kept with each photo. You don't have to do that yourself at all.

See the **Date taken,** item in the navigation bar. Double-click on it (or click the little arrowhead) to expand the date listings. You will see your photo history spread out in the navigation bar. You can find any date, you may need to expand a year or month to get there.

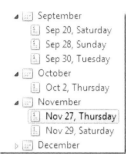

So you can find photos by the date they were taken or in your organization of folders.

But even if you remember making a folder with a specific name, you might have trouble locating it amongst all the others. Fear not! If you know the folders name, or even just part of it, Photo Gallery can help!

Up near the top right corner there is a search box – it says **Find a photo** faintly. If you want to find a folder, click on

 in the navigation bar, then type the folder name or part of it in the search box. Viola, the pictures from that folder (or all that match what you typed) appear in the main window.

Neat! But, as they say in the TV commercials, **there is more!** If you are willing to put in a little effort in the organization of your pictures, you can make locating any one even easier. I am talking about "tagging". Just as you used to write on the photo boxes or envelopes, or on the back of the pictures, to identify what the picture shows, in the world of digital pictures, you can accomplish the same with tagging. But…..

If you noticed the title of this blog had a "1" in it. Ha, that was planning. I will discuss more about tagging and finding your pictures in the sequel to this blog entry. I hope some of this has been of interest and use to you.

Find your photos 2 – tags

9/21/2009

Tags are one of the most useful features of digital images. Tags make finding a photo really easy. With the date being automatically recorded and maybe some additional fixed data, the photographer does not have to worry about that data. Tags are different. Tags need to be assigned manually. That sounds like more of a chore than it actually is. This blog is about finding pictures, but since you need to assign tags first, I will start with that task. Windows Live Photo Gallery recognizes two types of tags: *people tags* that identify persons shown in the photo, and *descriptive tags* that are used for everything else. In this blog, I will stick to just descriptive tags, leaving people tags for another day.

Descriptive tags can be assigned during the import process. That is easy when groups of photos cover the same subject matter – that is very often the case. Once the pictures are on the computer, tagging is easy in Photo Gallery. There are several ways.

Assigning a tag.

After importing, the pictures are now in separate folders as you grouped them. You can find them by folder or date. When a group is shown in the gallery, you can right-click the group name (shown in the picture here with a red pointer), and click **Select all**. Of course,

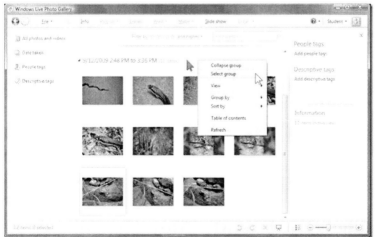

you can select a group the same way you select files in Windows Explorer. Naturally, you can just select one photo at time as well.

Once the photos are selected, click **Add descriptive tags** in the Info pane at the right. As soon as you start typing in the text entry box a little menu scrolls down ad shows all existing tags that start with that letter or letters. If the tag you want exists, just click on it and press Enter. You are done.

If the tag is a new one, finish typing and press Enter.

If this isn't easy enough, there is another quick way to assign an existing tag to one or more selected photos. Display the list of tags in the navigation pane – just click on **Descriptive tags**, scroll the list so you see the one you want, then drag the selected photos to the tag (with the pointer on any of the selected photos, press and hold the left mouse button to drag). Make sure you see the little **Apply ...** message as illustrated here:

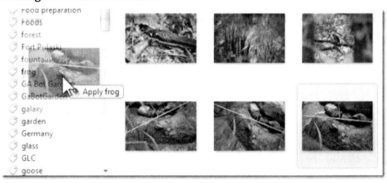

Easy enough? So let's get back to the subject of this blog.

Finding photos by tag.

Again there are a number of ways.

1) In the gallery you can display the thumbnails in different order. The default display is auto. Click there and one of the options is **Tag**:

You can then scroll your gallery and see the thumbnails arranged by tags.

2) Click on the name of the tag in the navigation pane (with descriptive tags expanded, you may need to scroll the list).

Oh, yes, you can select more than one tag! Hold down **Ctrl** as you select the tags you want.

3) You can find tagged photos with the search tool.

In you have selected a particular folder, or date, search will only show the photos in that selection. And yes, you can select several folders in the navigation pane the way you can select individual items – hold down **Ctrl** and click the folder or date.

Well, I trust that I convinced you that tags are an excellent tool for finding your pictures. In my next blog I will discuss People tags – really, really neat!

Find your photos 3 – people tags

10/8/2009

When I show of space photos and come to a picture with an astronaut, it helps to be able to tell who it is. All my life I have been a space fan. So my photo collection contains a number of astronomical and space program photos, a few from NASA, some showing astronauts. Windows Live Photo Gallery people tags really come in handy to find photos of people and to be able to tell who the people are.

But first I want to tell you how to go about tagging people. An earlier blog covered *descriptive tags*, now it is time for *people tags*. When you have a picture showing people, just double-click on the thumbnail image to bring up the photo full size. If the **Info** pane is not open, click **Info** in the menu bar. Windows Live Photo Gallery immediately checks for people. If it detects a face, it announces **"Person found - Identify"** in the Info pane.

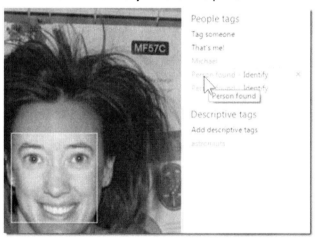

When you move the pointer to a "Person found" listing, the picture is dimmed with just the detected face highlighted like in the illustration here. In this picture one person has been tagged already.

Clicking on the highlighted face brings up a dialog with all the names of your friends and people tags that you have already assigned. This makes it easy to just click on a name to complete the tagging. If it is

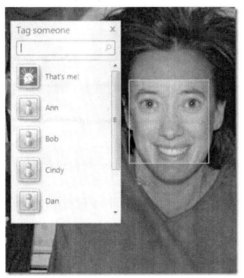

a new name, use the text entry box at the top to enter the persons name.

If Photo Gallery misses a face – it detects only full front, level faces – you can just click **Tag someone** and draw a box over the face. The tagged name is now listed in the **People tags** section in the navigation pane.

Finding People

There are two easy ways to find people.

1) Scroll through the **People tags** list. The tags are shown in groups. **Favorites** – if you have used that group – is one. **Other contacts** for

people in your contact list and **Other People** are the others. Just expand the list to see them. Click on a name and all the pictures with that person show up in the gallery pane.

2) Click **All photos and videos** in the navigation pane (or the folder
that you want to look in) and type the name you are looking for in
the search box. Photo Gallery displays the thumbnails that have a
word that starts with whatever you typed either in a tag, caption or
file name.

That's all it takes to find your photos showing tagged people!

One more nice feature: As you show pictures full size in Photo
Gallery, move the pointer to a face. A small label is displayed
showing the name.

You can give your
presentation confidently,
knowing that you can
quickly name your
friends in the pictures.

Illustrations in this post use NASA photo S125-E-006596 (12 May 2009)

Find your photos 4 – star rating

10/13/2009

Star ratings! Another way to find your photos using Windows Live Photo Gallery. There are so many options! In previous posts I blogged about how to find the folders, finding by the date the pictures were taken, by descriptive tags, and people tags. Now another neat method: star ratings. We all have pictures that we are very proud of and eager to show off to friends. Rating photos provides an option to identify those special photos. This does not mean that your rating system has to match anyone else's idea of what is outstanding, just yours. In fact, you don't have to base your rating system on "quality", it can really any classification that has just five classes.

When you select one or more thumbnails, or you have maximized a specific photo, down toward the right, in the **Info** pane, you can assign a **Rating**. Of course it helps to make up your mind beforehand about how you  want to rate your photos. So work your way through the pictures that you want to rate. Choose a star rating, or skip photos if you don't wish to assign any rating.

Once you have made rating assignments it is easy to find your photos.

Finding rated photos

In the main pane of Photo Gallery, at the top, there is a **Filter by** command. Just click the star rating you want to find.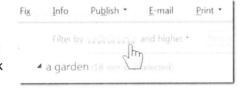

There is also menu for setting the option as shown here. You can select a rating and all those higher, or a rating and all those lower, or just a specific star rating.

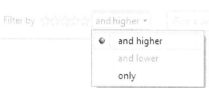

Click the rating star and the pictures with that rating are shown in the main gallery pane.

But there is more!

Select a folder or folders in the navigation pane and the star rating selection brings up only the rated photos from those folders. Here is an illustration of four-star only photos from just two folders: Remember, to select individual folders, hold down the **Ctrl** key while clicking the folder names.

Now, when your boss walks in, click **All photos and videos**, select five-stars only , and click **Slide show**. Show off just your best!

Find your photos 5 –using Search

10/27/2009

Previous posts covered finding photos in Windows Live Photo Gallery by file name, folder, date taken, descriptive tags, people tags, and ratings. This last installment looks at **Search**. Towards the upper right there is a text entry box with the faint text *"Find a photo"*. The explanation says "Type to start a text filter on your current view".

This short explanation just does not do justice to the power of this search option. "Find a photo" searches **file name**, **tags**, **caption** (title), **author**, and **camera** for matching text. Any words or numbers in those fields can be searched. This makes this a very powerful way to narrow down a search.

You start the search by selecting the general area in the navigation pane – **All photos and videos** for a universal search of your photos known to Photo Gallery. However, more likely you want a narrower group, maybe by location or date, or with selected tags. Next you can also filter by rating. Then you type the text word or words to look for.

Say I am looking for a four-star rated jpg photo of a goose taken in 2009:

1) Select 2009 in the navigation pane.

2) Click on the fourth star in the rating field.

3) In the search box type "jpg" and type "goose".

By the time I got to "go" the search was already narrowed down to just the one photo.

You can include the period in front of the file name suffix (like **.tif** or **.jpg**) to avoid including a photo that might have the suffix in the title or a tag.

You must try this search option for yourself to really appreciate the power, ease, and versatility.

Note:

You can type a large number of terms in the search box. The displayed pictures haveto match all the terms that you type in the search box, so this is an **AND** search.

When you select multiple tags, dates, or folders, in the navigation pane, all of the matching pictures are displayed, so such a selection is an **OR** search.

Since you can combine navigation pane OR with star and search AND selection, you have a very flexible and powerful way to find the picture or pictures you are looking for.

Black and White Effects

11/9/2009

Windows Live Photo Gallery has a selection of tools for "fixing" – enhancing, correcting – photos. Included is a group of six tools for black and white effects. Maybe I should say more correctly "monochrome" effects, because two of them are "Cyan tone" and "Sepia tone".

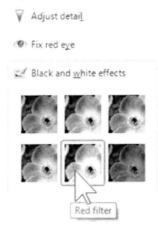

The effects go well beyond "fixing", they allow you to create images of different moods, pictures that are not just a representation of what you saw, but what you want to share with the viewer. The sepia tone creates images that evoke old times. Cyan abstracts a photo to a cool, formal image.

The other four are black and white effects. The first, "No filter", translates the photo to the gray tones that we find normal. It shows how a photo would appear when printed in a newspaper. Then there are three color filter effects, yellow, orange, and red.

Back in the days of black-and-white film photography, these filters were quite popular. I still have a collection of them – various sizes for different lenses – but now, with digital photography, I don't need the actual filters, the effects can be done with a click of the mouse. (The Undo option removes the effect – it is easy to try one after another.)

The yellow filter darkens blues and greens slightly. The orange filter deepens these effects. Blue skies are made darker, bringing out clouds more prominently. Green foliage is darkened while yellow and red colors of flowers are made lighter. The most dramatic color effects are achieved with the red filter.

Photo by Justin Keck

Here is a pleasant picture of Death Valley, California, showing the desolate landscape, the valley and the Panamint Mountains beyond. The mountains are some twenty-five miles (forty kilometers) away. The atmospheric haze makes them appear blue. We are used to that and associate that appearance with distance. The sky has just a few wispy clouds. Since the photos here are already in black and white, you can't fully appreciate what it looks like in color. So take a look at the cover where this picture is shown in color.

Now take a look at the dramatic picture that the red filter creates:

The sky is very dark, almost giving the picture the appearance of a night scene. The distant mountains seem much closer. The mood is totally different from the original color photo.

See what you can do with your photos. You might like what you can achieve.

Adjust detail – Sharpen and reduce noise

12/17/2009

Windows Live Photo Gallery has a collection of tool sets for "fixing" – enhancing – your photos. One of these is "**Adjust detail**".

There are two controls, **Sharpen** and **Reduce Noise**, to help you make the best of your pictures.

Pictures, or parts of pictures, can be unsharp, fuzzy, blurry, because the subject is out of focus or because either the subject or the camera moved during the exposure. All the picture detail was captured but it spread out and isn't where it belongs. So can the **Sharpen** control restore the picture to what it should be? Not quite. Like spilled milk, a blur is very difficult to undo. The sharpen algorithm in Windows Live Photo Gallery enhances edges. The dark side of an edge is made a bit darker and the light side lighter. The human eye perceives this a sharper. In the film days of photography, this came to be known as "acutance". If you have a picture with a large amount of detail, the **Sharpen** control can be used to make the photo look crisper. WLPG does the sharpening in real time, you can see the results instantly as you move the slider.

Double-click on a photo in the gallery to bring it up to fill the window. If the toolbar is not displayed on the right, click **Fix** in the menu bar. Click **Adjust detail**. Note how the picture is enlarged. You can position the displayed portion by dragging in the picture. You can adjust the zoom with the mouse wheel or the zoom slider at the lower right. Here is are three successive views as the Sharpen control is moved:

As you sharpen more fine detail gets the sharpening treatment and the picture becomes progressively unsatisfactory. The image will look grainy or noisy. To much sharpening is clearly detrimental. Nevertheless, let's take a look at what even over-sharpening has achieved. Here are the before and after images:

The picture on the right is the result of sharpening. It is clearly more satisfactory than the original. In the print reproduction here, you may not see the effect as clearly as you would in the actual photo.

Most digital photos will benefit from some sharpening. How much to sharpen is a matter of your judgment.

Now the other control, **Reduce Noise**. Photos taken at the highest ISO settings will show noise. The camera amplified the light signal to such an extent that electrical noise will become increasingly apparent. This picture here (top right on facing page)has noise added artificially.

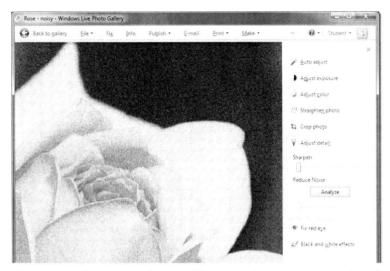

The noise reduction mechanism does just the opposite of what the sharpening tool does. It finds pixels that are significantly different from neighboring ones and averages them out. To reduce picture noise click the **Analyze** button. WLPG will take a moment and apply its best guess noise reduction. You can then use the slider to lessen the amount of noise reduction (move it left) or increase the amount. Reducing noise will make the picture look softer. Here is the rose picture with the default noise reduction:

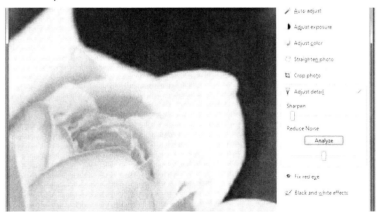

Powerful tools these are, as Yoda would have said. Use them with caution.

Live Spaces and Blogs

Spaces –
Your "mansion in the sky"

2/16/2010

With your Hotmail or Windows Live e-mail account, you get more than just a mail box. You get a cornucopia of services – a veritable "mansion in the sky". This mansion can be a very private place or you can have elaborate public spaces, with rooms for just your friends and family, and still have some private nooks just for yourself. You have a photo gallery with a multitude of public and private wings – your Photos album pages. There is a "reading room" – the Spaces page with many options for blogging, slide shows, news, even videos. There is also an attic, the SkyDrive, for storing odds and ends. The "foyer" has bulletin boards showing what you and your friends have been up to. There are even "doors" to step into your friends mansions. There must be places you have not explored yet, so let me be your guide. Of course, I can't show you around your mansion, so I will use a friend's grand place to illustrate. I will also get away from the mansion metaphor. It is a good one, but can't describe the full array of goodies at your finger tips.

So first an overview. When you are logged in to your online mail page, you are also logged in to your Windows Live account. At the top of the browser window there is a row of links:

You see these links whenever you are signed in even as you visit other Windows Live sites. These links lead to your own pages. Some of your services can be accessed by clicking the "More" link.

As you can see, the drop-down menu offers many additional links.

The first link, "Home", gets you to your home page, or the foyer in the mansion metaphor. This shows your top mailbox contents, and a variety of other information. The Options link allows you to customize this page. But not today, we are still doing the whirlwind tour.

The next link in the top row, "Profile", opens your profile page. Lot's of information here. We will skip this and the next two pages, "People" – your contacts, and "Mail" – your Hotmail page.

"Photos" opens your main page showing your albums.

Not all your albums will be shown. You can see them all by clicking "View all" Since you are signed in, you have access to all your albums. Some albums may be open to the public, everybody on the Internet, others may be shared with friends or just private for yourself (the little lock indicates that it is yours alone). For now, we will visit just two of the pages shown in the "More" menu. Look at "SkyDrive". This page is quite similar to the Photos page, except it shows all you folders. The photo albums are shown with picture icons, the others with folders icons.

Here also, "View all" will display all your folders and albums.

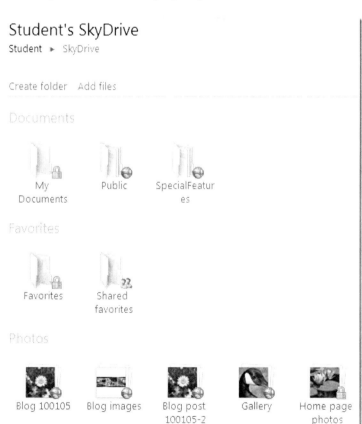

In SkyDrive there is a distinction between albums and folders. Albums are for photos and can reside only on the primary SkyDrive page. Folders contain files and folders. Any subfolder created inside an album or inside another folder is just a folder. Albums can be displayed on the Spaces page. Windows Live Photo Gallery can upload pictures to albums. Folders cannot be displayed or uploaded to, but you can add "files". Since this is getting a bit complex already, let's leave the details for another time.

The last place on this visit will be to your Space. This is your public website. You can choose to keep most of it private. You can have some fancy public pages. I already mentioned some at the start of this tour. Look at the site my friend, "Student", presents to the public.

You can visit the actual page at "**studentsa.spaces.live.com**"– In the online blog post, the picture links to the site. There is much to explore. There are pictures, albums, a video, a book list, stock quotes, weather, blog posts, …. So much to see and learn.

A view of the Spaces page of "Student":

This view shows the site as it looked on February 15, 2010. Folks change, improve, update, modify their sites all the time. On your visit it probably will look quite different. That is the charm of Spaces, you can keep updating your site easily and thus often.

Spaces – Your showplace on the Web

2/17/2010

Your Spaces page is your face on the Web, this is how friends, family and strangers see you. It is easy to shape your face to your personality. Windows Live Spaces pages contain "modules". You can select what modules to show, how they are arranges, design themes for the page and more. Let me show you.

 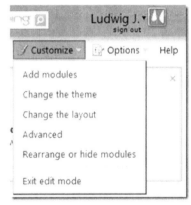

When you log in to your Windows Live account, you are taken to your Home page. I like to get to my Spaces page from my Profile page – it is really a gateway page to my pages and to those of all the people in my network. The link to the Spaces page is on the left under the profile picture. On the Spaces page in the upper right is the link to **Customize**. This is where you can let your imagination roam. If you are new to your Spaces page, you will want to start with **Add modules**. You will find a large number of options. They are shown in nine groups:

- **Featured modules**
- **Social**
- **Photos, music, and video**
- **Blog**
- **Lists**
- **Gadgets**

- **Xbox Live**
- **Other**
- **Space tools**

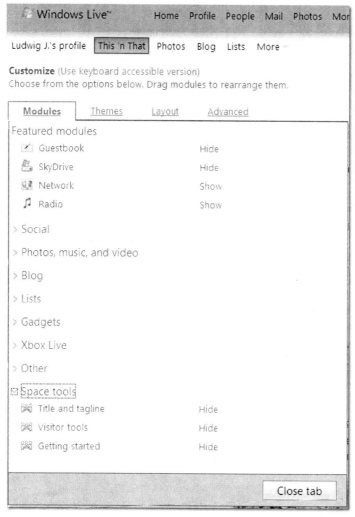

I discussed some of the options for Themes and Layout in another blog: *Show off your Photos on your Spaces page*, see page 60. Take a look.

Here is a really neat module: **Book list**.

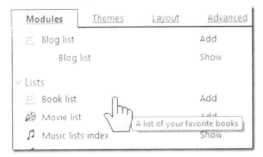

To add the module click on the **Book list... Add** line. In Spaces, you click **Add** to add the module. A new line will be added showing the module with the **Hide** option so you can "hide" the module from your page. After adding the module (and saving), the module will show on your page:

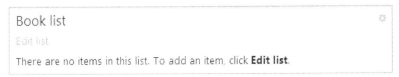

Next comes the impressive fun! Click **Edit list**.

Of course, this being a new list, there is nothing on it. So click **Add book**. In the next window you are requested to enter the book title, and you can enter the author and/or ISBN number if you know these. Here for this exercise, I just typed the title of one of my books. The Search link searches the Internet for information about books with the information that was entered. The results show little images of the book covers. My book was one of those found.

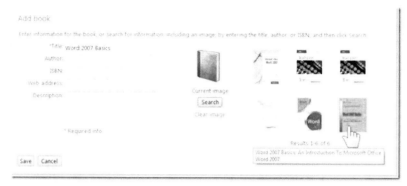

Clicking on a book image in the results causes the other fields to be filled with the correct information. A couple of click to get back, and there is the book list on the Spaces page.

There you have it. Not only is it really easy to put up a list of your favorite books, the list provides links for obtaining more information on each book. For this book it takes you right to the book's page on Amazon.com.

Arranging pictures in your Live Spaces Photo site by drag and drop

4/24/2009

Oh my! I heard from far and wide, from friends and strangers: I want to re-arrange my Spaces Photos pictures, how can I do it? All I did was mention Photos and Slide Show in my last blog, and somehow struck a nerve. If you have not seen it elsewhere, here it is again: Our friends at Windows Live had been working hard to provide the tools and functions you want. **Yes, you can re-arrange the order of your pictures by just dragging and dropping.**

Here is how it is done:

First make sure you have Silverlight installed. If you don't have Silverlight, or are not sure, go to this site:

www.microsoft.com/silverlight/get-started/install/default.aspx

It will tell you if you have it, and let you install from there if you don't.

Now, sign into your account and go to the folder in your Photos site where you want to customize the order. Click on **Sort by:** Then select **Arrange photos.**

In the new window you will be able to drag and drop – arrange your photos the way you want.

Note how the photo you are dragging fades out and photos will spread apart and make room as you drag a photo to a new location.

What could be neater?

Happy now?

Show your Photos on your Spaces page

6/1/2009

Spaces nicely makes various features readily available:

Compared to the Spaces main page the **Photos** page is rather utilitarian. It is efficient but plain:

If you want to show off your photos in a more spectacular way do it on your main Spaces page. You can add up to six photo modules (at present). Log into your Spaces page and click **Customize** over toward the right. The menu allows you to change the layout, the theme, and to add modules.

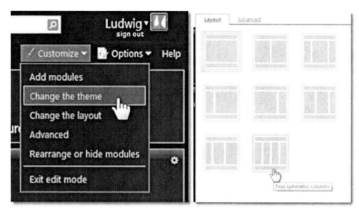

You may want to first set your page layout. The eight options may seem meager, but you can really do a lot of arranging in any of the layouts.

In the **Customize** menu select **Add modules**. Scroll down a bit and notice the **Add** in the **Photos** section. Click it to add a module. Once you have reached the limit of six the Add control disappears.

Make sure that for each photos module it says **Hide** – indicating that **Show** is presently in force. Save your settings.

Now the fun begins. In the **Customize** menu click **Rearrange or hide modules**. You can arrange the modules by dragging them into the position you want. Take a look at a couple different layouts of my "gallery":

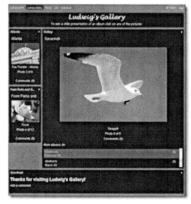

Here are two more versions:

 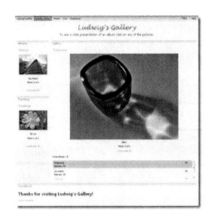

You can drag the modules around until you are happy. In any of the layouts, you can drag a module to the top or bottom area and it will be added full width as shown in the first example above. Any of the areas can hold multiple modules.

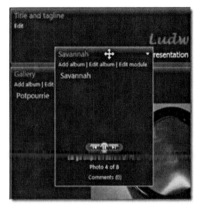

There are many options, see a couple of the menus here:

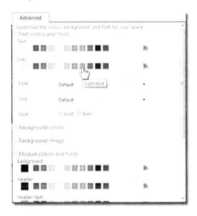 

There is more!

When a viewer clicks on any of the pictures, she is taken to the gorgeous Windows Live slide viewer.

On each module there is a picture control. If you leave that set to play then in most browsers the photos will play through the album. You can select the speed (**Edit module**). Visitors also have this control available and can stop and start the show or advance to the next or previous picture.

You have more than six albums? For each module you can select which albums to include. In the illustrations of my gallery above the right two show the **Album picker** turned on so visitors can select the album to view.

So you see there are a huge number of variations – one is sure to appeal to you as being just right. You may visit my photo gallery at **ludwigkeck.spaces.live.com** to see what I think is just right for me. Of course, by tomorrow I may have changed my mind and modified my page.

Have fun!

Show off your Photos in your Spaces blog
6/5/2009

My Gallery Pages

Of course, you can show off pictures in your blogs. That way you can have a great deal of control of the appearance of your site.

Here is an example:

This site uses a blog entry to display the title pictures of individual albums. To make this even more attractive a link is assigned to each picture. The link leads to the Windows Live slide show of that album.

Here is how to do that:

Bring up the slide show for the album in your browser. Copy the address. Then in preparing the blog click on the picture you inserted (with **Insert picture**) and click on **Insert hyperlink**. Enter the address of the running slide show.

On my desktop, the process looks a bit like the picture here:

The browser (left background) is running the slide show for the selected picture in the blog. I clicked in the address bar and with **Ctrl+C** copied the address. Then I selected **Insert hyperlink** and with **Ctrl+V** placed the address into the **URL** field of the **Edit Hyperlink** dialog. This is done for each picture.

The finished blog is published and there you have it.

If you want a better idea about how this works go to "Ludwig's Gallery 2" at **ludwigkeck2.spaces.live.com** – and take a look – be sure to click on some of the pictures to see how the links work.

This gallery is for illustrative purposes and makes no claims to artistic merit.

Moving Spaces Photos files and folders

9/24/2009

Every so often most of us find that our arrangement of "albums" or folders no longer seems to fit our needs. So, you want to "move some furniture around". Well, things don't work the same way up in the clouds as they do down home. You go to your Space Photos and you try to drag a folder from one place to another, or into another folder. All you get is that nice:  - "Unavailable". You cannot re-arrange the folders or move one folder into another by dragging.

However! You can move contents from one folder to any other. You can move a subfolder, a folder inside another folder, to any other. Here is how:

Moving a photo

Sign in to your Spaces account, go to Photos, the folder where the picture is. Click on the picture. When the picture is displayed there is a menu bar above it.

There is a command **Move**. Clicking on this gets you to something like this illustration on the right:

Click on the destination folder – you may have to scroll.

You get something like this:

If there are folders inside the destination folder, they are also shown as in the previous step. Clicking steps you into that folder.

When the correct path is displayed, click on **Move this file into ....** The file is moved. **Any file in that folder with the same name is overwritten without warning!**

Bummer: You can only move one photo at a time.

Moving a folder

This has to be a subfolder. This will not work for the primary folders that are displayed in **Photos**.

Go to the folder and click on it. The menu bar above the thumbnails will have a **More** option at the end. Clicking this get to something like this:

Click the Move command. The following steps are the same as explained above, but instead of moving a single picture, you will be moving the entire folder, with all subfolders!

Bummer: Only primary folders can be included in a module on your Spaces site.

However, you can link to a slide show of the pictures in a subfolder in a blog post, as explained in the blog "Show off your Photos in your Spaces blog".

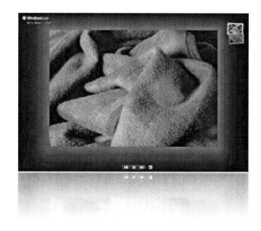

Uploading folders to SkyDrive

2/20/2010

There are times when I want to upload not just a few pictures but a whole collection to my SkyDrive. Turns out that this is not as simple as I first imagined. Here is the procedure I attempted. You may have run into this yourself. I logged in to my Live account, maneuvered to SkyDrive, created the folder that I wanted for my collection. It opened up the Add files dialog. I dragged the folder from my local Pictures library. Here is what happened:

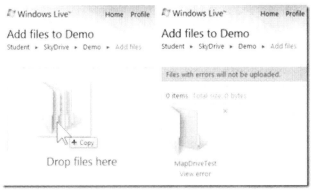

This does not work. You cannot add folders, just individual files.

A short while back, Mynetx posted the solution to this dilemma. The work around is mapping the SkyDrive folder into the computer so it looks like just another drive on the system. His procedure is described in detail in the post **How-to: Connect Your SkyDrive in Windows Explorer** (on mynetx.net). I will recap the procedure here – this procedure is for Windows 7. It works pretty much the same in Vista.

Note: Only an album or a primary folder in the SkyDrive can be mapped as a local drive. The entire SkyDrive cannot be mapped, subfolders cannot be mapped.

Log into your Windows Live account. Obtain the cid of the SkyDrive, that is everything after the hyphen and before the next period. See the illustration here:

Open Windows Explorer (**Start – Computer**).

Open **Map network drive**. Select the drive letter you want to use. Enter this string into the Folder: box **\\docs.live.net@SSL** (see illustration here).

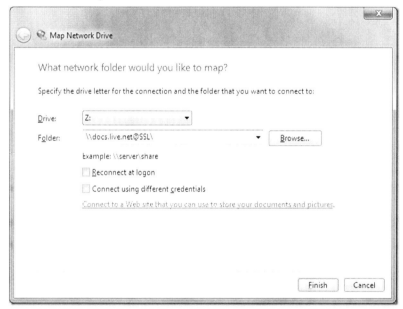

Paste your cid number after the string followed by a back-slash and the name of the folder on the SkyDrive you wish to map. The folder must exist, the name may contain spaces.

Click **Finish**.

A dialog will show that a connection is being established, followed by a log in request.

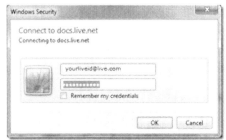

Login with your Live account credentials. Moments later a Windows Explorer window open with you newly mapped drive.

It will show in Windows Explorer as illustrated here.

If you get repeated login requests or a notice that the drive could not be found, try this: Turn off your firewall, repeat the mapping, then turn your firewall back on.

Now back to copying a folder up to the SkyDrive.

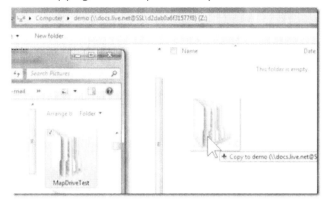

Use the newly mapped drive just like any other folder on your computer. In the illustration here, I show dragging a folder to the mapped drive. Since this uploads files to the SkyDrive, it will be slower than normal copying. Your upload speed is determined by the type of Internet connection you have.

So, what else can you do? See this:

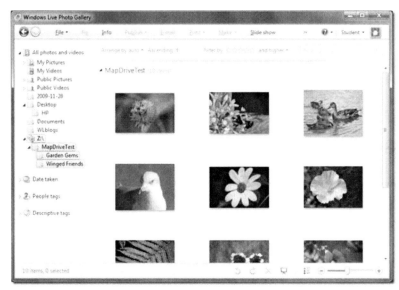

You can include the mapped drive in Windows Live Photo Gallery.
You can work on the photos just like any other, but keep in mind
that it involves down-loading and up-loading, so the process will be
slow. Of, course you can use the mapped folder just like any other,
copying, moving things around. Files operate just like any other
(except in Properties there is no Security tab) – all the file properties
are there:

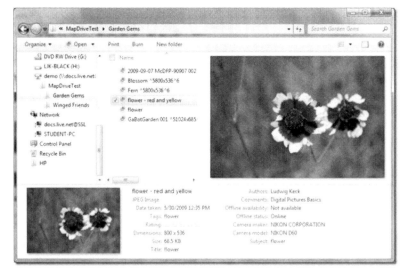

Note of caution. Some folks, like me, have pathological computer setups. I have two operating systems installed on my machine in dual-boot configuration. I use different user names in the systems. Some drives are commonly available. Some files on those drives will be created by one user, some by the other. The ownership of files from the other system (which is, of course, not operating) will show up as "Account unknown" – uploading such a file to a public folder on the SkyDrive could be a security breach. Windows 7 is smarter than that and will not upload such files (you do get a warning).

One other note of caution: I have had problems with mapped SkyDrive folder being marked for "reconnect at logon" mostly on my Windows 7 machine where security is tighter.

Mapping several SkyDrive folders is no problem. I have mapped SkyDrive folders belonging to different users (Connect using different credentials) without problems. The firewall remembers not to interfere on subsequent mappings.

Mapping SkyDrive folders has been very useful to me, makes many chores very easy. A tip of the hat to Mynetx.

Using fancy fonts in your blog post

1/9/2010

Sometimes you would like to make something really stand out by using a fancy font. As you prepare your blog post in Windows Live Writer, the Font command in the menu bar allows you to select from a wide range of fonts that are installed on your computer. So click on the "Font" **A** and select the font you like:

Danger, Will Robinson!

[Look it up.] There is a trap right here! Here is how it might look in your Windows Live Writer Edit pane (formatted for your specific blog site):

> Using fancy fonts
>
> Sometimes you would like to make something really stand out by using a fancy font. The Font command in the menu bar allows you to select from a wide range of fonts that are installed on your computer.
>
> *That seems to solve one of your problems.*

So what's the problem? Looks ok, doesn't it? Plough right on. Next you want it larger still. The font control only goes to 36, bummer. You manually type in "72" – doesn't work – bummer, bummer. Then you remember there is an **Edit – Paste special...** option. So you open Word, type the text, format it to the font and size you like. Select it and copy it. Click **Edit**, then **Paste special...** :

Click **Keep Formatting** and presto, it looks like this:

Problem solved? You post your blog and feel smug.

Danger, Will Robinson!

Your problem is not solved. Here is how a couple of friends might see your blog:

So what went wrong? Just because you have "Vivaldi" font on your machine, does not mean that everyone else does also. Your friend's browser will substitute another font if the one you specified is not installed on that computer. Font size typically works ok.

Moral: Do not use unusual fonts, they may not be available on your viewer's computer and your post will not look like you intended.

Workaround? If you must have an unusual font and size, paste it in as a picture:

Insert it as a picture!

Happy posting!

Fun with Live Writer and Photo Gallery

1/5/2010

Windows Live Writer offers some fun options and so does Windows Live Photo Gallery. Here I will start in Photo Gallery and select some photos. Clicking the **Make** command offers several options. What I want to demonstrate is **Make a blog post**.

Now if you selected at least three pictures you get the dialog shown on the right.

Inline Images is nice, but choosing **Photo Photo Album** is more fun. Live Writer opens, looking about like this:

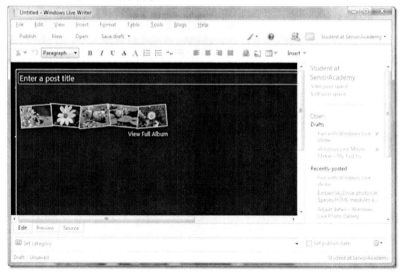

Quite pretty! Clicking on the picture display gets **Photo Album** tools including **Album style:** This selects how the display looks in the blog. The default is **Spread** as shown at left.

If you have selected a large number of photos the **Fan** option might be nice. **Scatter** is always interesting.

There is a **Change cover picture** option. You have to click this repeatedly to find the display you like best.

The **Edit Photo Album** tool allows modifying the album, you can add or remove pictures, and you can specify the album name. Using this tool is optional, of course.

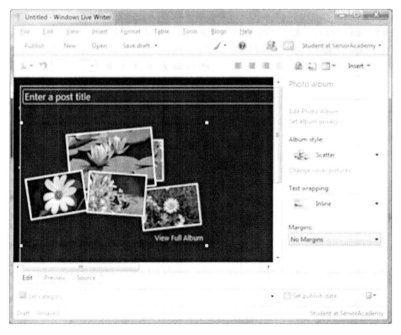

If you do make changes, the album name is required. You can resize and reposition the array. The **View Full Album** link will be placed as shown.

When you are ready to publish your blog post, just click **Publish**. If

you have not named the album a dialog will request you to do so. Two things happen next: The album is created in your SkyDrive and the blog is published to your Spaces page. (Yes, there are other options, but here I just go with these.)

This is fast and easy! Nice integration and interaction between Windows Live Photo Gallery, Live Writer and SkyDrive!

Want to see the slideshow of this demo album?

Go to this Spaces Photos page: **studentsa.spaces.live.com/photos**

The click on **Blog post 100105-2** to go to the album for this blog.

Finally click **Slide show** to see the show. Enjoy!

Embed SkyDrive photos in Spaces HTML modules and other websites

1/3/2010

Spaces offers a rich variety of options and when you really need full control you can add HTML modules. Embedding photos in an HTML module from your SkyDrive folders is not at all hard to do. The procedure described here will seem quite familiar to you. It works with the Spaces HTML modules and can be used with other websites. Here we will use Windows Live Writer so you wont need to write any HTML code yourself – you'll see why shortly when you take a look at the code produced by Live Writer.

If you do not already have an HTML module on your Spaces page here are the instructions for adding one:

Adding an HTML module to your Spaces page

Log into your Live account and go to your Spaces page. Over toward the right side click **Customize**. Then click **Add modules** on the drop-down menu.

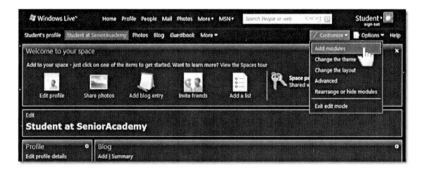

In the modules menu scroll down to the **Other** group and click on **Custom HTML**. Click **Close Tab** and drag the module to the place on you page where you want it.

Click on the down arrowhead (upper right of the new module) and select **Settings**. You can now specify the title of the module and how it is displayed.

Here we show **Use full width** for the module. Click **Save** and your new HTML module is ready for adding your text and illustrations.

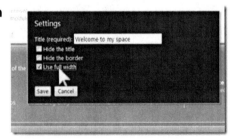

Click **Edit** (below the
module title). A text entry
window opens that expects
HTML code. This is where
we take another tack.

Preparing your HTML code

Open **Windows Live Writer**. This is an easy way to prepare the code
for your HTML module. Here you can set up text as you like – that
we won't discuss in this blog. Here I just want to describe how to
add photos. You can't just paste a photo into the HTML module. The
photo has to be available somewhere on the Internet and you need

to link to it. Your SkyDrive is a good
place for keeping the photos.

Maneuver over to you SkyDrive and
the photo you want to insert. I like to
do this in a new tab in my browser.
Click on the photo so it is displayed
all by itself in the browser. Now right-
click the photo. Click **Copy** in the little
menu.

Click in the text window in Live Writer and paste the picture with **Ctrl-V**. While the photo is selected make the desired settings for size, placement and the other option.

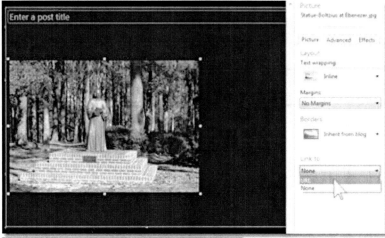

Now go back to the browser showing the photo. Click in the address bar to select the address of the photo. Copy the address with **Ctrl-C**. Back to Live Writer. Find the **Link to** control – it will say **None**. Click on it and select **URL**.

The Hyperlink menu will open to allow you to define the link to the photo – this is optional but you most likely will want to allow the viewer to see your photo full screen. Click in the URL entry window and paste the address with **Ctrl-V**.

You can specify the picture title and some other options. Click **Insert** when you are done.

Complete the text and maybe other photos in Live Writer. When you are finished what remains is transferring the HTML code from Live Writer to your Spaces HTML module.

Transferring the code

Below the edit window in Live Writer click Source. You will see the complete HTML code that describes all the details as you set them up.

Select the entire text with **Ctrl-A**. Then copy everything with **Ctrl-C**.

Now back to your HTML module. Click in the window and paste the HTML code with **Ctrl-V**. The Live Writer source code window and the HTML module are illustrated here. Obviously, yours will look a lot differently.

Now above the HTML module text window click **Publish**. Your HTML module will look exactly as it does in your Live Writer. Be sure to save. Mission accomplished.

Reading the instructions here probably took longer than it will take you to add your first picture to an HTML module. After the second one, the procedure will seem second nature. It is jst a matter of copying and pasting. It really is that easy.

Here is the Spaces page (at this stage of editing) as others would see it:

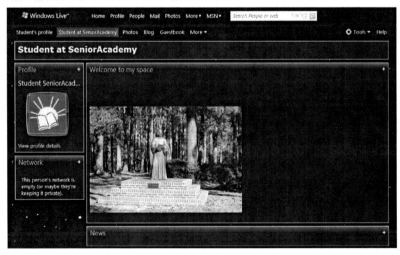

Windows 7

Windows 7 – Paint – 1

5/20/2009

In my recent posts I have chatted about some of the new things in Windows 7. Now I have come to **Paint**. Paint has been given a major rework. There was a challenge recently in the Clubhouse* to tell about "must-have" software. Well, looking back, I find that I use Paint again and again to process screen captures when working on textbook manuscripts, classroom presentations, and most of my recent *This 'n That* posts. There are other tools to do this, but on my computers they seem to all have fallen into disuse.

Paint is of course a simple, unsophisticated drawing program and does a fine job for that. I can get some of the simple tasks done in Paint in less time than it takes for some of my fancy "image processing" programs to spin up. But, back to what's new with Paint.

The Paint program in Windows 7 now sports a Ribbon and has the "new family" look introduced in Office 2007. There are a few more tools, the status bar gives better information, many of the customary tools have been improved in subtle ways.

There is much to like in the new Paint. In my next post I will show off a couple of the neat new features. Unfortunately there are a couple things that were not carried over from the previous versions of Paint: "Copy to" and transparent "Paste from".

* For my readers who are not "club members": The Clubhouse: It's where everyday Windows users like you share their stories and tips and learn cool stuff.   Find it at **clubhouse.microsoft.com**

As I said, I like to use it for screen capture processing. For example: In illustrating how to copy pictures to another folder, I might want a picture like this:

This involves a screen capture ("Print Screen" key) then cutting out the desired portion. The "print screen" operation will capture the image of the pointer only under some conditions, which don't ever seem to be when I want it. So, I just paste a pointer image in. Takes just a few seconds using the old XP or Vista Paint, and it requires "Paste from" in transparent mode and then "Copy to" to save the cutout picture.

In the new Paint the workaround is a bit more complex. It goes like this:

1) Set up the condition you want to illustrate then press **"Print Screen"** (on some machines this may be a key combination like "Function"+"Print Screen"). You will capture everything but the pointer (some situations excepted when you actually can get it all). Now paste it into Paint.

2) Open Paint and click **Paste** (or do **Ctrl+V**).

3) In another instance of Paint, Open a picture of pointer images. Here is one of mine:

4) Click the little down arrow under **Select** and click **Transparent selection**.

5) Now select the pointer image and click **Copy** (or use **Ctrl+C**).

6) Bring to the front the instance of Paint with the captured screen image.

7) Click **Paste**, and here also select transparent mode (like in step 3).

8) Now move the pointer image into place.

9) Select the portion of the image you want. Click **Copy** and paste your image into the application where you want it. It is really faster than reading about it here.

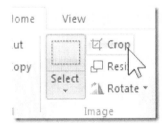

10) If you want to save the image, in Paint click **Crop**. The selection will now become the image in the Paint window and you can save it.

OK, how many people are out there that need this kind of operation? Maybe seventeen others besides me? No wonder Microsoft dropped transparent "Paste from". But notice transparent pasting works just fine from one Paint instance to another. And "Copy to" can be accomplished with crop and save.

So why do I describe this elaborate process? Well, the technique might come in handy for you. ***Have fun with Paint!***

Windows 7 – Paint – 2

5/21/2009

In my last post, I complained about some of the changes in the new Paint program. Today it's time for unabashed admiration of the improvements and features in Windows 7 Paint. I will chat about a few of the new things and a few of the old features, and do it in the form of a walk-through demonstration – if it is reminiscent of a classroom demonstration you guessed right, have a seat.

Paint is still a single-canvas drawing program. It now sports a Ribbon and has a "Paint button" like the "Office button" in Office 2007.

Click it and you can select Open – the right pane shows recent files used in Paint. Clicking Open gets the normal Open dialog. Here I opened a picture of a gull.

We will have a bit of fun with this picture. Let's see what that suspicious looking gull is thinking by adding a "thought" bubble as is customary in comics. But first, there isn't enough room for that. As

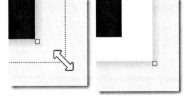

is customary in Paint, we can resize the canvas by dragging a resize handle. In Paint, these are a bit small and unobtrusive.

When the pointer is released, the added area of the canvas takes the color shown in the Color 2 (background) color box, here it is white.

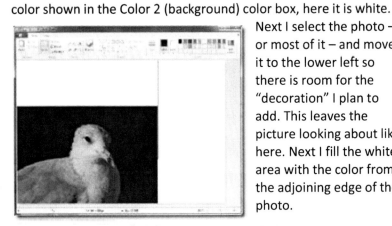

Next I select the photo – or most of it – and move it to the lower left so there is room for the "decoration" I plan to add. This leaves the picture looking about like here. Next I fill the white area with the color from the adjoining edge of the photo.

Then I select the "Cloud callout" and draw the shape by dragging a rectangular area. While that shape draw rectangle is active – so long as you don't click outside the

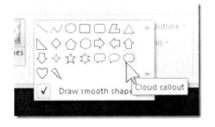

area – you can change the size, the location (by dragging), the color and brush for the shape, the color of the fill. And you can see the result by just hovering over the tools in the ribbon.

There is no way to convey the neat way these tools work, you just have to try it yourself! I set the size to the maximum setting, the Outline to "Crayon" and the Color 1 to orange.

So what is the gull thinking? The text tool is just as neat. You can put the text box anywhere and compose the text in the font and size then drag it to the proper location. You can edit and modify the text

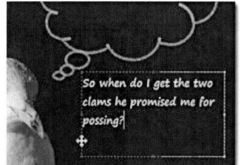

just like in a word processing program, by selecting and modifying it.

Well, now we have our masterpiece, but I am not quite done.

I want the final picture to be just 640 pixels wide. Here the new Paint has made the resizing chore much more easy to use.

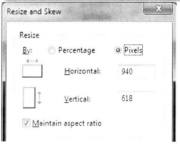

The resize tool now has a "Maintain aspect ratio" check box and the option to resize in pixels, not just in percentage. By the way, the resize tool can be used on the whole canvas, or, if an area is selected, on just that area. Click on the image for a better view.

So there you have it. We demonstrated loading a file, resizing the canvas, the new shapes and the new features of the text tool, and finally resizing the whole picture. One additional comment: The default format for Paint is now PNG to save the image without degradation.

The new Paint program is really much improved and a pleasure to use. Enjoy!

Windows 7 – On-Screen Keyboard

5/17/2009

Windows 7 has a much improved on-screen keyboard, here is a view:

The buttons – keys – are larger than in the Vista on-screen keyboard. Compare the actual-size cutouts:

So folks who need the on-screen keyboard will have an easier time with it. There is another useful improvement: The characters that you get when you hold down the shift key (or click the Shift button) are shown on the keyboard at all times – just like on a real keyboard.

The on-screen keyboard is one of the few instance when you can actually have two windows active – the keyboard and the application that you are typing into.

There is one really useful new option called Text Prediction. As you type on the on-screen keyboard the top row is populated with buttons that contain words that complete what you started to type. Here is an illustration, say that in your text you want to enter the word "feature". When you click the "f" key the top row shows:

for	from	five	four	first	fifty	forty	found

If there is a button there for the word you want just click it and it completes the word in the document. If the word is not there, click the next letter. For example "e".

Still not there, so click the "a" key and get:

Now the word is included in the row of word buttons, click it and the word will be completed in the text you are typing. It even inserts the space following the word.

I find the on-screen keyboard especially useful when I need to type in a foreign language – something I don't do often enough to remember the layout of the keyboard. Having the layout in front of me helps to find the right keys. For example see here the French and Russian keyboards.

Keep the on-screen keyboard in mind, there may come an occasion when you will find it useful.

Windows 7 Sticky Notes

5/13/2009

Sticky Notes in Windows 7 have grown up. No longer is there a Sticky Notes gadget like in Vista, it is now a program residing in the **Accessories** folder. When you click on the program name the first time, you get a little yellow notepad and you can type your note. It will look something like this:

On inspection, you see that it is just the same as in your Vista days. Except for the

resizing handle in the lower right corner. Indeed the note can be resized as you like. So you can write rather lengthy notes. You are still limited to the "scripty" font in just one size.

Now when you want to write another sticky and click on the there is a pleasant surprise. In Vista you got to a new page on the same pad. With Windows 7 Sticky Notes you get another fresh new note on the desktop. You can clutter up your Windows 7 desktop just the way you do the one the computer sits on. Isn't that grand?!

Since Sticky Notes is a regular

program, but with multiple windows, it gets its entry on the Taskbar. When you hover on the icon you get the thumbnail – and if your eyesight is tad better than mine, you can read the text of the last note.

Hover on the thumbnail and magic: All the open windows are "glassed" and you see the sticky notes on top.

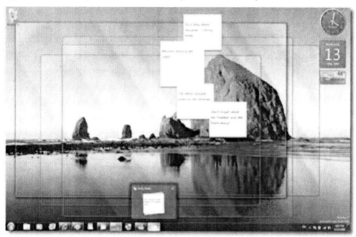

Grander!! Clicking **Start** gets you the Start menu, of course. Having started Sticky Notes will have the program on the start menu. The little right arrow gets you this:

The right pane has an option "**New Note**" but does not show the open notes. Betcha this is temporary! Now if you click **Start** and

type "sticky" there is a list on the Start menu of the last three notes:

Any other neat trick? Hovering the pointer on the "**Show desktop**" button removes the notes from view and "glasses" out the other

windows. Of course the ⨯ in the upper right corner closes, removes, that note.

Enough for today. Enjoy!

Windows 7 - Gadgets

5/11/2009

In Windows 7 the Sidebar is gone, but Gadgets are there. Now Gadgets need not reside in the Sidebar and can be placed anywhere on the desktop. In Vista when you dragged a Gadget out of the Sidebar it could be placed anywhere, but some would enlarge to display more information. The Weather Gadget would give a three-day forecast. In Windows 7 it still does. Gadgets that have such features now have an additional control. When you mouse to the

right of a Gadget a little control panel appears that allows you to close, resize (on some), set options (the little wrench) or drag the Gadget.

So when you click on the you get the larger option, like here.

Of course, now the little control panel changes to:

Gadgets are considered part of the desktop and do not disappear when you mouse over the "Show desktop" box or click on it.

Oh, you want to know how to get to Gadgets?

Well, when you click **Start** and type "sidebar" you get:

Or you can type "gadget" – even quicker as it puts right at the top, just press Enter.

Programs (1)

Desktop Gadget Gallery

Curious why "sidebar" gets you there? Turns out gadgets reside in a folder called "Windows Sidebar". Why? Something about reptilian brain stems or... oh, never mind.

And the third option – never fear, there are always three options – just right-click on a empty space on the desktop. Note the second to last option in the menu:

One of the Gadgets is no longer available in the Gadget selector: Sticky notes, that is now in programs.

Windows 7 Magnifier

There is much in Windows 7 to make it easier for us older folks. A very happy surprise was the Magnifier in Windows 7.

The new Magnifier has a "lens" option (the default) which magnifies an area around the pointer. For us seniors this is much easier and more intuitive than the previous version. It works just like that real magnifier sitting next to my telephone. Those little fly specks in front of folders in a navigation pane now look like the little arrow heads that they are. More importantly, it is now much easier to place the pointer where you need it.

The lens size can be changed as well as the magnification. There is a full screen mode – the lens is now the size of the screen and looks at a portion of a much larger desktop. Also quite nice. The old "docked" mode is still available for those who have mastered that approach. Something my students in class always struggled with – and gave up on.

Be sure to try the new Magnifier – it is a very nice improvement.

Windows 7 WordPad – File types

6/13/2009

The Windows 7 WordPad program is a much improved, actually all new, text editing utility. Take a quick look:

WordPad now features a "Ribbon" to make all the options and controls readily available. It also sports an "Office Button"-like control to bring up the open, save, print etc options.

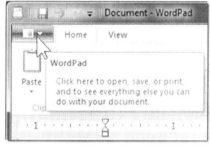

Today I want to concentrate on file formats. In the Vista WordPad you had basically just two

choices: It could open and save Rich Text Format (RTF) or plain text format (TXT) files. The new Windows 7 WordPad has a wider array of file type options.

Here are the "Save as" options as they appear in the main option menu. The default format is still "Rich Text document" (RTF).

Notice the next two entries: "Office Open XML document" and "OpenDocument text". The names may be new to you. Here is the big news: the file extensions are DOCX and ODT. Yup, same as you get in Office Word 2007 under "Word Document" and "OpenDocument Text". This is the good news, there is, however, also some --- interesting news.

Word 2007 can open the Windows 7 WordPad files saved as DOCX, ODT, or RTF. No problem.

Windows 7 WordPad can open Word 2007 files saved as DOCX, ODT, or RTF but with some limitations. Here is an illustration, note the warning line:

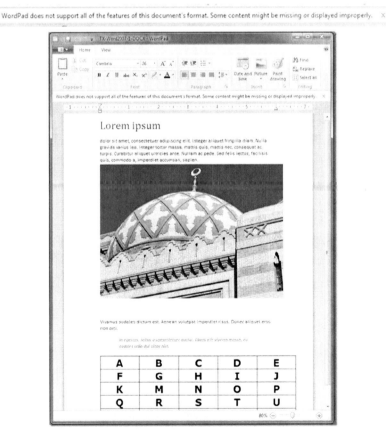

WordPad does not support all the features. In the original Word 2007 document the title is underlined as is the colored text above the table. This is true as well in the other two formats, ODT and RTF. I have opened some rather complex Word 2007 documents in the new WordPad and in all cases the document was at least fully readable. Some of the little niceties are not supported as well as the more complex features. For example, WordPad cannot display an embedded spreadsheet. The table shown in the above document can be seen in WordPad just fine. The contents of the cells can be edited although there are no table tools. When saved and opened again on Word 2007 the table shows the modifications and works as expected.

There are significant differences in the way the information is stored inside saved files. This becomes noticeable when you just look at the files. I created a Word 2007 document with just text and an image and saved the file three ways: Word Document (DOCX), RTF, and ODT. I did the same using Windows 7 WordPad. Then I opened the Word 2007 DOCX file in WordPad and re-saved it as three different file types (with a new name). The picture here shows the files, you can figure out from the filenames which is what.

WIN7 TEST ▸ WordPad Test ▸ Plain

Name	Date modified	Type	Size
TP-Word2007-1-DOCX.docx	6/12/2009 8:13 PM	Microsoft Office Word Document	219 KB
TP-Word2007-1-DOCX-WordPad-DOCX.docx	6/12/2009 8:31 PM	Microsoft Office Word Document	1,203 KB
TP-Word2007-1-DOCX-WordPad-ODT.odt	6/12/2009 8:32 PM	OpenDocument Text	1,568 KB
TP-Word2007-1-DOCX-WordPad-RTF.rtf	6/12/2009 8:31 PM	RTF File	4,420 KB
TP-Word2007-1-ODT.odt	6/12/2009 8:14 PM	OpenDocument Text	213 KB
TP-Word2007-1-RTF.rtf	6/12/2009 8:14 PM	RTF File	8,187 KB
TP-WordPad-1-DOCX.docx	6/12/2009 8:29 PM	Microsoft Office Word Document	1,203 KB
TP-WordPad-1-ODT.odt	6/12/2009 8:29 PM	OpenDocument Text	1,568 KB
TP-WordPad-1-RTF.rtf	6/12/2009 8:28 PM	RTF File	4,420 KB

Notice the difference in file sizes – all these contain exactly the same text and picture. Some of the differences "under the hood" are quite fascinating to techies. The images are stored inside the files in different formats. For normal users this is of no concern.

To sum up: The new Windows 7 WordPad is a much improved and very useful text editor. It can open files saved natively by Word 2007. In turn, a Word 2007 user can open the WordPad files. Windows 7 WordPad cannot open the older Word DOC format files.

A user learning WordPad will have little trouble when encountering Word 2007 – the programs are very similar in appearance and the way they work.

There are some other neat new features in WordPad that I will leave for another blog.

Windows 7 WordPad – insert picture
6/24/2009

The new WordPad in Windows 7 makes inserting pictures quite easy. On the **Home** ribbon there is an **Insert** group:

Click on **Insert – Picture** and you get a **Select Picture** dialog that lets you choose the picture just like in other applications.

The picture is inserted at the *text insertion point* – the flashing vertical cursor. It is placed at the left margin and, if it would exceed the text width, it is scaled to fit from margin to margin.

The other conventional modes of inserting work just as well. You can copy the file in Windows Explorer with **Ctrl+C** and paste it into the WordPad text with **Ctrl+V**. Similarly, right-clicking on the file in Windows Explorer has a **Copy** command in the menu, and right-clicking in WordPad, at the place you want the picture, presents a **Paste** option.

And for the dragsters among us, you can drag a file from Windows Explorer into WordPad. Just hold down the left mouse button over the file and drag it to the place in WordPad where you want the picture. While outside WordPad you will see the file image (as shown below).

Once you are over WordPad the pointer changes to the insertion pointer like here.

WordPad does not support text wrapping around a picture. If the picture is small you can set it left, centered, or to the right margin with the Paragraph controls or by right-clicking on the picture and selecting **Paragraph**. This last option also lets you set the picture at a specified distance from the margin with **Indentation**. You can also resize the picture, again by right-clicking on it of clicking the picture and clicking on the down arrow below Picture on the ribbon.

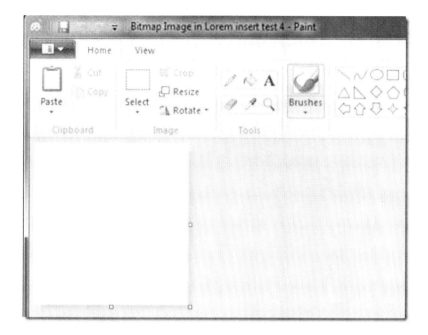

The other neat option in the **Insert** group on the **Home** ribbon is **Paint drawing**. Click on that and Paint opens.

This mode of Paint lets you do just about anything you can normally do in Paint. The **New, Open, Save** options will not show when you click the **Paint button** (but **Paste from** works if you really need to load some image). When you have created your image, just close Paint and the image is inserted into WordPad. You can then resize it and place it just like with other pictures.

The new WordPad has a lot of new and improved features. It is not a full-featured text editing program like Word but it does a respectable job. For simple documents it is quick and easy.

Windows 7 Calculator

10/29/2009

Some neat new features are offered
in the Windows 7 Calculator. At first
glance, it looks just like a cheap little
calculator, but look a little deeper
and you find a powerful tool!

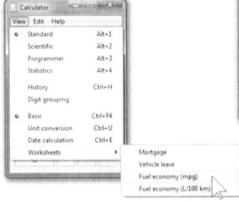

Click on **View** and the
new uses become
apparent. First, there
are the different modes
– **Standard** (as shown here), **Scientific** – with trig and the other
functions expected on such a calculator, **Programmer** – even 64-bit
binary!, **Statistics** – just the basics, but nicely done.

It saves and displays the history of your calculations – every entry.
You can even go back and make corrections.

Digit grouping in the results, with commas separating the thousands
(in the US version).

Unit conversions are offered for some of the basic measurements.

Lastly, there a "**Worksheets**" for making mortgage, lease, and
vehicle fuel economy calculations.

Calculating fuel economy

To illustrate the use of the new calculator, let's quickly check my
car's mpg (miles per gallon). Here is a page form my car log:

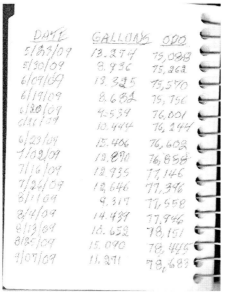

To calculate the fuel economy we divide the distance traveled by the fuel used. The first fill-up here was at 75,088 miles on the odometer, there were 14 fill-up, the last at 78,683 on the odo.

The fuel amounts are added. The sum is copied (with **Ctrl-C**) and pasted in to the **Fuel used** text box.

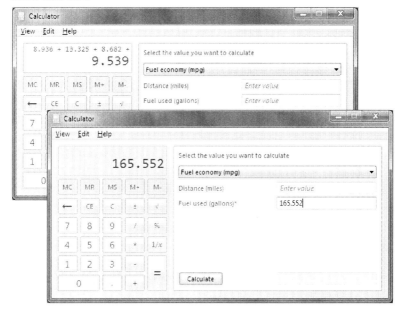

The last odometer reading is entered and the first one subtracted to get the distance. This is similarly copied to the **Distance** box. Click the **Calculate** button and the results are displayed.

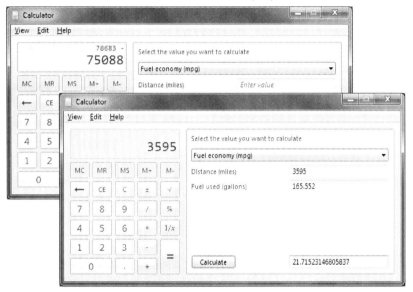

Selecting **View – History** allows reviewing – even correcting – all the entries made in the current session. You can even copy the entire history (**Edit – History – Copy history**) and paste the data into another application.

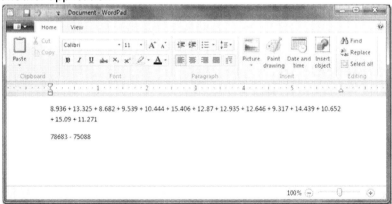

Neat, yes?!

Word 2010

Word 2010 – Background Remover

11/18/2009

Office 2010 brings some fine changes. Here I want to show one **"WOW"** change in **Word 2010** – The picture background remover tool.

Loading a picture is pretty much as it was in Word 2007, but when **Picture Tools** comes up the most prominent item is on the left end of the ribbon: **Remove Background**.

For pictures like the one here, where the background is very distinct, the remover tool works essentially automatically.

It offers a cropping rectangle. There are tools for marking areas – to keep or to remove. The area to be removed is colored over. Clicking **Keep Changes** applies the selections.

But there is more. Selecting **Wrap Text – Tight** wraps text to the remaining part of the image, not to the selected crop area. You can even apply a shadow to the remaining image like this:

For this example I did not have to use the **Mark Area to Keep** or **Mark Areas to Remove** tools. I guess that will keep for another day.

Is this great or what?

Word 2010 – Insert Screenshot

12/14/2009

Another new feature in the **Office 2010** lineup is the **Insert Screenshot** tool:

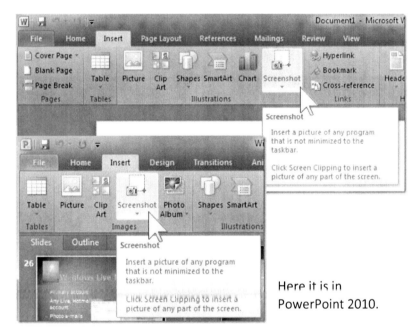

Here it is in PowerPoint 2010.

Clicking on that control opens a small menu showing all open windows. Minimized windows are not included.

Even though the application windows may be all over the desktop and stacked behind each other, the menu shows them all. Clicking on one of the little images instantly brings a picture of that window into Word (or other Office 2010 application) and pastes it full width. You can then resize and reposition the image as you wish.

Of course, there is more!

Click on **Screen Clipping** on the bottom of the small menu, and the Word window is minimized, the screen is "grayed" out and you have a cross-shaped drawing pointer for defining the area to be clipped. Position the cross-shaped pointer and press and hold the main mouse button to drag a rectangle over the area to be clipped. The selected area shows normally, that is, not grayed out. It looks like this screenshot on the next page.

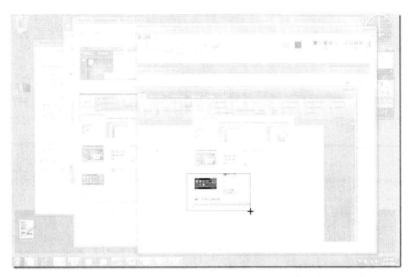

When the mouse button is released, Word comes back up and the clipping is inserted.

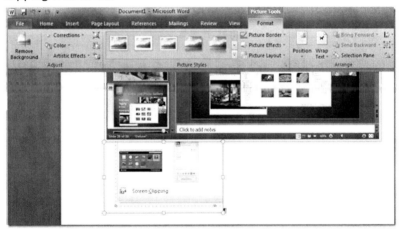

Neat! The process is the same in **PowerPoint 2010, Excel 2010, Outlook 2010** ….

So there you are. Nice new features in **Office 2010**!

Miscelleneous

Changing the drive letter of USB devices

4/15/2009

Like most folks, I have a good number of USB devices. External hard drives for backup and to store files, flash drives for pictures and presentations – it goes on. Windows is great at recognizing the drive when it is plugged in and it assigns the next available drive letter. Windows remembers that letter and uses it the next time – if it is available. Sometimes things are plugged in already. When you plug a drive in, the letter it used the last time might be already in use. No problem for Windows – it just finds the next free drive letter and off we go.

Well, that can cause all kinds of annoyances. The backup program won't recognize the drive if the letter has changed. Ditto for Windows Live Photo Gallery, Word in its Recent List, etc. and on. I used to unplug some devices and try to connect them in different order. Sometimes this worked, most of the time it didn't.

When a drive is labeled as G: and the previous time it was F: it is a problem. So how do you change the drive letter to what you want? Or, better yet, how do you assign each device a letter different from all the others?

Here's how:

Use Computer Management to reassign the drive letter for a device to whatever you want (within limits). Windows will use this letter the next time the drive is connected.

Click **Start** and type *computer management* – actually I usually just type *manage*.

Computer Management will show up at or near the top of the Start menu. Click it. Give UAC permission to continue.

In the Computer Management window look in the navigation pane on the left and find – under **Storage** - **Disk Management**. Click it.

The drives will be listed in the center pane with nice graphics depicting each drive.

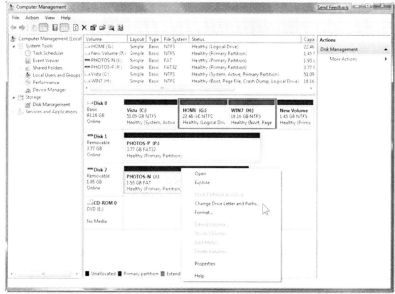

Right-click the graphic of the drive whose letter you want to change. In the drop-down menu click **Change Drive Letter and Paths...**

In the next dialog (shown here) click **Change...**

In the **Change Drive Letter...** dialog click on the down arrowhead
next to the drive letter and select the letter you want in the
dropdown menu. Only available letters will be shown.

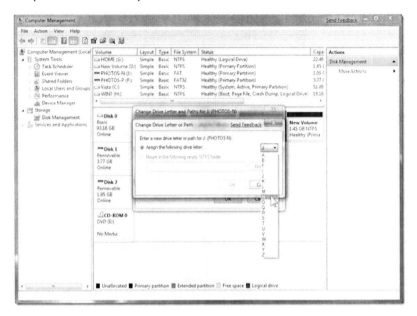

One final warning that
changing the letter might
affect programs – click **Yes** –
you do want to make the
change. After all, affecting the
programs is why you want to do it in the first place.

I have started to name my drives with the desired drive letter right
in the name. Like **PHOTOS-N** and **PHOTOS-P**. This way I can
remember what the drive letter should be, next time Windows
forgets – because I messed up somehow.

Assigning drive letters this way has been a real help. Now I can
concentrate on what I am doing and don't need to worry –
Windows Live Photo Gallery finds my pictures, when I click on a
Word recent list entry the document opens because Word finds it.

It even gives me time to write blogs!

Sharing Pictures of Documents – A big little problem

4/13/2009

My student Cathy came up with this problem. She attached a scan of an old letter to an e-mail. The recipient complaint that it was unreadable. She had sent pictures that way many times and everyone seemed happy enough. Not this time.

Here I am using a "simulated" old letter. Viewing an enlarged portion of the original shows that it is quite readable (if you pardon the Latin), but the letter as received is quite bad as shown below.

Nullam in orci. Aenean
lacinia, ligula quis porttitor
arcu et nisi. Duis dictum

Nullam in orci. Aenean
lacinia, ligula quis porttitor
arcu et nisi. Duis dictum

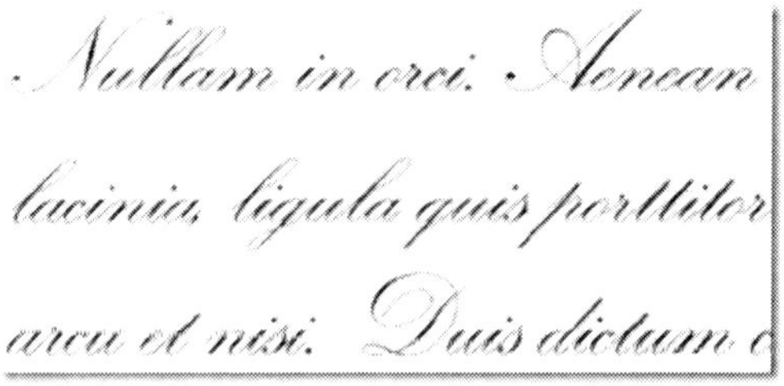

So what happened?

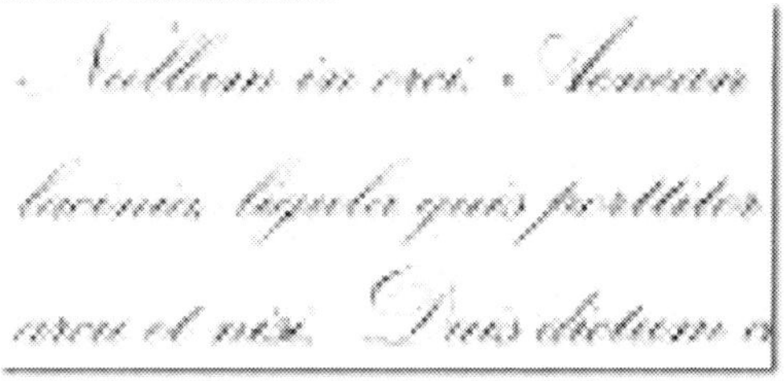

She was using Hotmail. To attach the picture, she used **Attach – Photo**, just like she always does. Hotmail handles this in a way that many users don't realize or don't remember: Hotmail automatically scales the picture down to limit the larger dimension to 600 pixels. This is not usually a problem with photos of people or things, but a scanned document, originally page size, now becomes reduced to where it may no longer be readable. In this case, the original was 1700 by 2066 pixels – the file size was 531 KB. Hotmail reduced it to 494 x 600 pixels, file size just 32.4 KB.

Why?

A smaller file is faster to upload and to download. It takes less space on the Hotmail server. In days when Internet access speeds were not as fast – think dial-up – and when storage space was much more limited, this was the thing to do. It is still a good idea. Although Hotmail storage is now no longer an issue, upload and download speed still is, especially when you share a number of picture.

So what is the solution?

There are several:

1) **Hotmail** – Send the picture not as a **Photo** but as a **File**. This may not be easy to remember, and it certainly may lead to lengthy upload and download times.

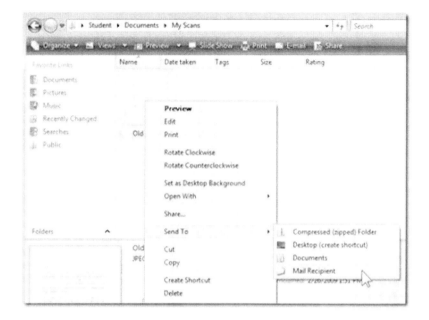

2) Send To – Rather than attaching to an e-mail, start by selecting the item in **Windows Explorer**. Right-click and choose **Send To** - then in the submenu click **Mail Recipient**.

An **Attach File** dialog opens to allow you to select the **Picture Size**. This will remind you that the file can be reduced, or sent full size. The mail client then opens so you can compose your e-mail. There is an additional advantage: By selecting the attached picture first you won't forget to do so. I often need to send an "oops – I forgot to attach the picture" e-mail with the forgotten attachment.

3) Windows Live Photo Gallery – In Windoes Live Photo Gallery select the picture then click **E-mail** in the toolbar. It then works just as described in 2) above.

4) SkyDrive – The best way in my opinion. Upload the file to your **SkyDrive** – you can make it private and inform your recipient of the file. This eliminates the download at the recipients end when the e-mail comes in. So much easier! The recipient can then download the file at a convenient time.

Don't forget: Hotmail **Photo** attachments are quietly resized. A good thing most of the time – but can be quite an annoyance for scanned documents.

Index

CPSIA information can be obtained at www.ICGtesting.com
Printed in the USA
BVOW011418050213

312465BV00009B/190/P

9 781450 583206